Cute and Easy
CAKE TOPPERS

Cute and Lovable
Cake Topper Characters for Every Occasion!

BRENDA WALTON

About Sugar High...

Fredericksburg, Virginia-based Brenda Walton launched **Sugar High Inc.** in the summer of 2011 to celebrate her love of fondant modeling and all things cute!

What started as a simple plan to create a cake for her daughter's first birthday soon grew into a passion and unique talent for fondant modeling, and Brenda soon amassed a large and loyal online following with her cute and whimsical creations.

This is Brenda's first book, and she also teaches in-person at locations across the USA, Canada and Europe. **Sugar High** also recently launched a range of exclusive **'Bakedrop'** products – themed cake photography backdrops for the hobby or professional cake maker.

Find out more at:

www.sugarhighinc.com

First published in 2014 by Kyle Craig Publishing

Edited by Alison McNicol

Text and illustration copyright © 2014 Kyle Craig Ltd.

ISBN: 978-1-908-707-42-0

A CIP record for this book is available from the British Library.

Library Of Congress Cataloging-in-Publication Data - A catalog for this book is available from the Library of Congress.

A Kyle Craig Publication www.kyle-craig.com

Contents

Welcome!

Hi all!

Welcome to my first Sugar High book, Cute and Easy Cake Toppers!

I am so thrilled to bring you this sweet and fun collection of my favorite cute characters, and hope you will relax, enjoy, and especially have fun creating some little characters of your own!

I can't wait to show you my simple and easy techniques to help you create the details which will really bring your characters to life. When you look at your little character and it just brings a smile to your face, then you know you have just put yourself on that Sugar High!

My **Sugar High** journey began in September 2010 when I decided to try my hand at making my daughter's first birthday cake. I created my first 3 tiered, fondant covered cake with little butterflies and bees and simple flowers. Wow! I was hooked! It was love at first try! This simple, sweet, sugary goodness has put me on a Sugar High ever since!

I soon found that my true passion lay in creating fondant cake and cupcake toppers and so I now no longer make big cakes; instead I love to focus on bringing my ideas to life in fabulous fondant! I'm a huge kid at heart and adore all things cute, and just love to fill my work space with everything I love to help fire my imagination!

I am so very thankful to all of you who follow me and I hope you enjoy making your own cute creations!

Sending you tons of sugar love!

xoxo, Brenda

Fun with Fondant!

I personally prefer to use *Satin Ice* brand fondant when creating all of my fondant figures. I use all of their pre-made colors and will also mix these base colors to create others using their color mixing chart, which is on their website. If there is a color I am not able to mix, I prefer to use *Americolor* food color.

The temperature and weather will affect working ability so I like to keep my room temperature around 70-72 degrees, and on rainy days I use a de-humidifier in my room to help with humidity.

Tylose

For the larger pieces in my models (say, over 1.5oz of fondant being used) I like to add a pinch of *Tylose* (about ⅛ tsp) to help stiffen the fondant. I usually just take my ball and dip it once into the *Tylose* then work it through the fondant.

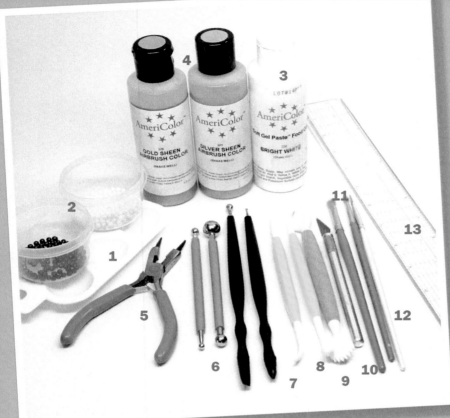

There are certain tools that I consider essential for modeling – some of which you may already have. These are the items that I would consider my 'essentials':

My Essential Tools

1 Paint tray
2 Dragees in 4mm size, black and white
3 *Americolor* Food Colors: white
4 *Americolor Airbrush Sheen*: gold and silver
5 Wire cutters
6 Ball tools in various sizes
7 Dresden tool
8 Boning tool
9 *Wilton* knife tool
10 Craft knife/scalpel
11 Paint brushes
12 Fine tip paint brush
13 Clear ruler

Shaping Rolling and Sticking!

There are quite a few other items used to help shape, roll, stick and mark your models:

1 Foam pieces for drying/supports (can be cut to size)
2 Edible glue* see below
3 4"x 2" cake dummies (to support figures when modeling)
4 4" and 6" cake bases
5 Rolling pin (acrylic)
6 White floral wire 22gauge
7 Skewers 6", 4"
8 Toothpicks
9 Floral stamens

* Edible Glue: I make my own edible glue by dissolving 1 cup boiling water to 1 tablespoon of Tylose powder.

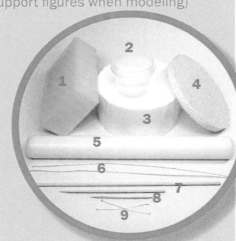

Cutters, Plungers and Tips!

I have a great selection of cutters to help cut out all the shapes required for my models. Plunger cutters are also wonderful for cutting and 'pushing' out very small shapes. Here are some of my most used:

Ateco brand cutter set - circles
Ateco brand cutter set - geometric shapes
Heart plunger cutters by *Ateco*
Flower plunger cutters by PME
Various tips by *Wilton*, #10 round, #12 round, #3 round and Grass

Making Faces!

Use the knife tool, or sometimes a circle cutter, to indent for facial features.

Use various size ball tools to indent for noses. From small 1/8" ball on up to 1/2".

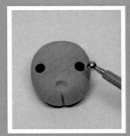

Use 1/8" or 1/4" ball tool then roll the same size black fondant balls for eyes.

Two different methods for highlighting eyes are white fondant OR dots of white food color.

Add shading on faces that is a few shades darker than the fondant color, AND pink for cheeks.

Add eyelashes using a fine detail brush, diluting brown or black food color with a touch of vodka.

Add freckles with the blunt end of a tooth-pick dipped into brown food color.

Eyebrows can be added using a fine detail brush with a touch of vodka and brown or black food color.

Measurements

Being based in the USA I favor **ounces** and **inches**, but for my European friends, here are a couple of handy conversion tables to help you follow my directions!

Ounces/Grams

Oz	g
.05	1.42
.10	2.84
.25	7.08
.50	14.18
.75	21.26
1	28.35
1.25	35.44
1.5	42.52
1.75	49.61
2	56.70
5	141.75

Inches/Centimeters

In	cm
1/16"	0.16
1/8"	0.32
1/4"	0.64
1/2"	1.27
3/4"	1.90
1"	2.54
2"	5.08
3"	7.62
4"	10.16
5"	12.70
6"	15.24

Areas
to
Shade

Adding shading to various parts of your creatures can really help add depth and character and bring them to life.

I use a *Petal Crafts* petal dust pallette - pictured - but I also own *Wilton*, *Americolor*, and several other brands of petal dusts, so use whatever you prefer.

Browns and darker shading can add depth to your models. Pay particular attention to: bends, hands, feet, muzzles, under ears, arm and leg seams.

Paws for Thought!

There are several tools that you will use regularly to create details for your limbs; usually the knife tool, dresden tool or ball tools, depending on the detailing required.

Roll fondant according to the limb shape needed.

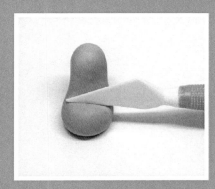

Add crease details with the back of the knife tool.

Bend limbs into simple angles and add in paw details.

1 Roll .80oz yellow into a 2" sausage, cut in half with cut end facing down. Insert a 5" skewer through one leg and toothpick through the other.

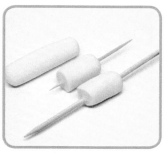

2 Roll .075oz yellow to a ¾" sausage and indent twice with knife tool to form toes.

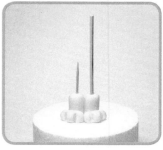

3 Insert legs into foam support and glue together in center. Also glue toes onto front of legs.

4 Roll 1.5oz of yellow into an egg shape for the body and glue in place on top of legs.

5 Cut out a blue 1" square, ½"thick. Roll and cut thin green strips and a small ball for bow detail. Glue to front center of bunny.

6 Roll .10oz yellow to a tapered sausage. Indent twice with knife tool, forming fingers at end of arm. Repeat for second arm.

7 Glue arms to side of body and onto side of present.

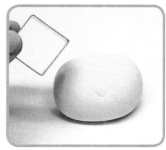

8 Roll 2oz of yellow into an oval for the head and indent with corner of square cutter to form nose, about a third way up the head.

9 Indent a straight line down from nose and use ¼" ball tool to indent for eyes.

10 Roll a ¼" green ball and flatten. Glue to top of neck area. This is for the base of the bow tie.

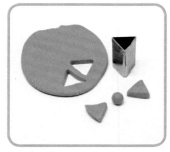

11 Cut 2 green triangles and roll a ¼" ball. Glue to front of green band around neck.

12 Glue head onto body, create (2) ¼" black balls for eyes.

13 Cut (2) 1" ovals in yellow. Pinch together one end and trim ¼" off other end. Glue both to head and each other, touching in the middle.

14 Add details with petal dust: yellow - creases, ears; pink - ears, cheeks, nose; green - bow tie; dark blue - ribbon on gift. Paint eyebrows and add white dots on eyes.

Tools

4½" and 6" skewers
1¾" circle cutter
⅛" ball tool
#3 round tip
Small triangle cutter
5 petal daisy cutters:
1¼", ¾" and ½" plain
leaf/teardrop cutter
Gold luster dust

1 Roll .10oz green into a 2.5" long sausage then flatten. Apply glue to fondant, and lay 6" skewer down and wrap around and roll. Trim to 2".

2 Roll green to ⅛" thick. Cut 2 medium daisies and 2 small daisies. Trim off 2 petals. These will form the hands and feet.

3 Roll a second leg to match the first, but no need for a skewer. Glue free leg onto skewered leg and then glue to feet.

4 Roll 1oz of blue to a 2" sausage. Flatten bottom and across the whole length to form jacket. Center on legs and glue into place.

5 Roll (2) .07oz tapered sausages to 1¾" long. Indent larger end with ball tool. Glue onto both sides of jacket for arms.

6 Roll and cut a ¼" x 2" strip of yellow. Glue strip to center of jacket front.

7 Cut 2 plain teardrop/leaf shapes, then use the #3 round tip to cut 8 buttons.

8 Glue teardrops to top of shoulders, large end out. Glue 4 buttons to each side of yellow strip. Glue hands to end of arms.

9 Roll .50oz of green into a 2" long sausage. Bend slightly and use the circle cutter at an angle to form mouth.

10 Roll (2) .07oz white balls for eyes, indent with ⅛" ball tool and roll black balls for eyes. Glue mouth on body and glue eyes to the top.

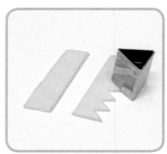

11 Cut a yellow strip ½" x 2". Use medium triangle as shown to create crown. Glue ends together and then glue above the eyes.

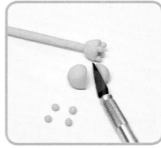

12 Repeat Step 1 with yellow and a 4.5" skewer for the staff. Roll ½" ball of yellow, cut off top third and glue to end of staff, cut side up. Roll (4) ⅛" balls and glue to top.

13 Roll ⅛" green balls for all ends of fingers and toes and glue on.

14 Paint crown, buttons and balls on top of staff with gold. Shade and blush.

Little Miss Mouse

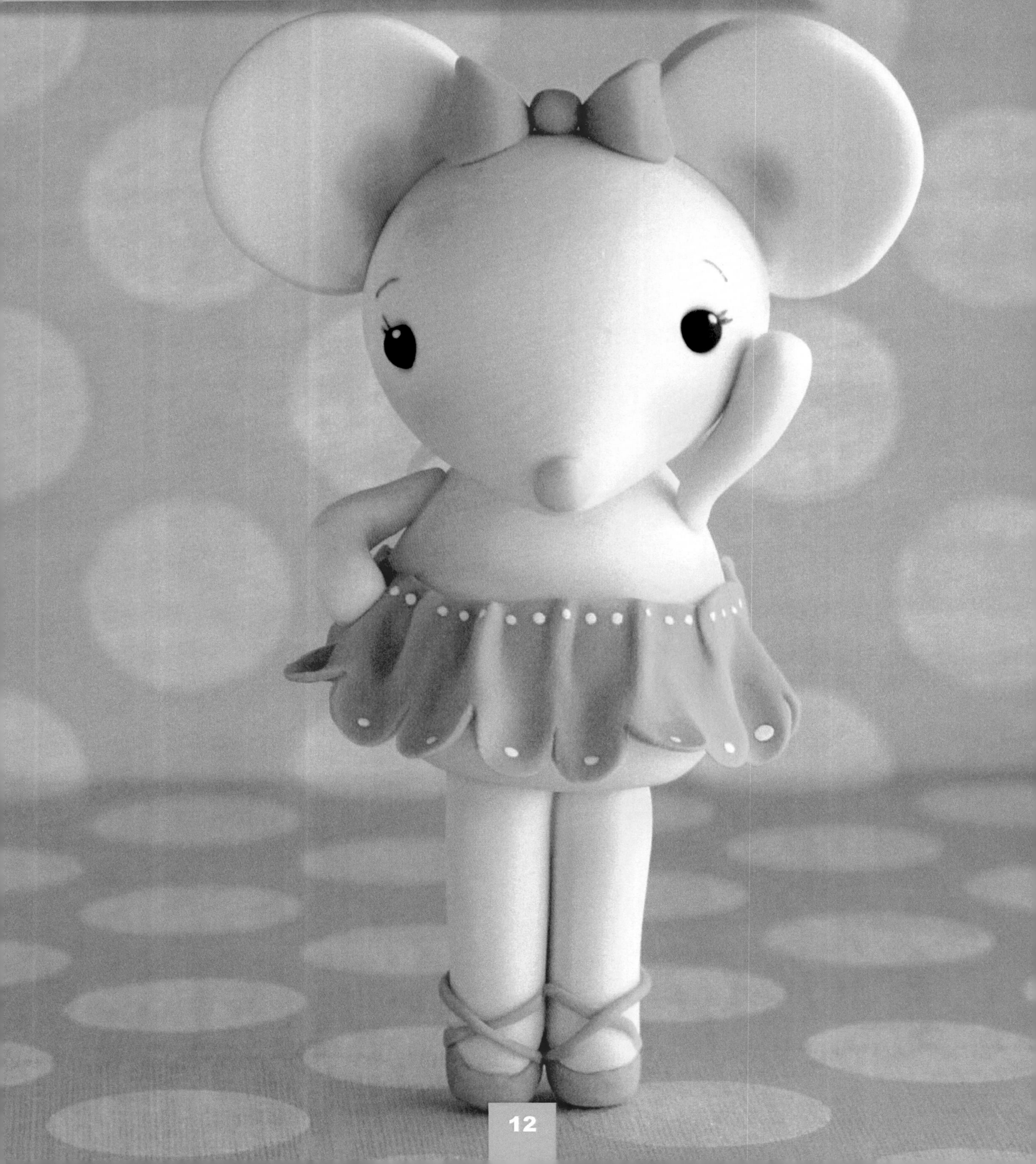

Fondant

Pink

Pale pink

Medium pink – pinch

Black

Tools

Toothpicks
5" skewer
2" scallop cutter
⅛", ¼" and ½" ball tools
1" and ½" circle cutter
Food color: white, black

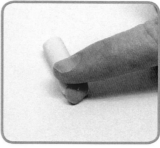

1 Roll .20oz pale pink to 1.5" sausage and cut in half. Roll ⅛" thick in pink and cut ½"circle for ballet slipper.

2 Glue ½" pink circle onto rounded end of sausage and roll to form. Insert toothpick through center. Repeat, inserting a 5" skewer into the second leg.

3 Place legs next to each other, glue in between and place on foam support. Roll 1oz pale pink body into an egg shape. Insert onto skewer.

4 Roll 1.5oz into teardrop shape for head. Indent tip of head with ¼" ball tool for nose and ⅛" ball tool for eyes. Add ⅛" black balls for eyes and ¼" pink ball for nose.

5 Roll 2" ball of pink to ¹⁄₁₆" thickness. Cut 2" round scallop. Use 1"circle to cut out center. Slice one side with blade.

6 Frill end with ½" ball tool. Use toothpick to lift and pinch pleats at each scallop.

7 Glue skirt around mouse body, with the seam meeting at the back. Glue head onto top.

8 Roll 1" ball of pale pink to ⅛" thickness. Cut (2) 1" circles. Using same cutter, cut out ¼" in. Use ½" ball tool to indent slightly in center of ear at cut end.

9 Glue ears onto head. The ears should align straight above leg position if viewed from the side.

10 Roll (2) .25oz tapered sausages for arms.

11 Glue left arm onto shoulder and onto side of face. Bend right arm slightly and glue onto shoulder and skirt.

12 Roll .20oz pale pink into long 2.5" strip for tail. Glue to bottom and have the tail curve up around skirt and glue onto back.

13 Roll a 1" ball of pink and cut (2) ¾" diamonds and roll an ⅛" ball. Fold diamonds over and glue bow onto center of mouse head.

14 Roll tiny pink strips and glue into an "X" to form laces. Paint white dots onto skirt. Add finishing details – cheeks, ears, creases, eyelashes and eyebrows.

Fondant

Grey

Red

Black

White

Yellow (pinch)

Tools

Toothpicks x 2
1" circle cutter
Cutting wheel tool
¼" and large ball tools
Small flower cutter
Small veining tool
#10 circle tip
Tiny heart cutter
Florist wire
Petal dust: black, pink
Food color: black, red

1 Roll 1oz grey and 1oz red into ovals. You will need 2 sets like this to make both the boy and girl.

2 Use largest ball tool you have and indent and roll in clockwise motion to hollow out center to a 2"opening.

3 Glue inside of red and place onto grey. Smooth out around edges to form together.

4 Use cutting wheel to indent line down the center of the back.

5 Insert skewer down center. Use cutting wheel to indent 3 lines across grey body. After both bodies are made place just touching each other.

6 Roll .50oz grey into an oval. Indent top half slightly to form face.

7 Use small veining tool to indent eyes. Leave ½" space between eyes for girl.

8 For boy's head use the ¼" ball tool to make indents for eyes about 1" apart. Indent mouths with small 1" cutter or open end of a piping tip. Glue heads on.

9 Roll ¼" grey balls for feet. Roll ¼" grey balls into 1" long tapered sausages for arms.

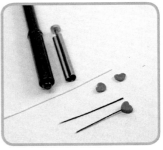

10 Roll red to ¹⁄₁₆" thick. Cut out 8 hearts. Cut (4) 2" floral wires and use black edible ink pen to color black. Glue 2 hearts back to back with wire in center to form antennae.

11 Roll ⅛" black balls into tapered sausages ¼" long for girl's eyes. Roll ¼" black balls for boy's eyes. Insert antennae.

12 Roll out 1" ball of black to ¹⁄₁₆" thick. Use #10 circle tip to cut out several dots and glue to back of wings.

13 Use a tiny flower cutter to make little flower for the girl's head. Add a second arm to the girl, if you wish.

14 Add shading. Black – edges of body, seams and top of head. Pink for cheeks. Paint black food color for lashes and eyebrows, and red for lips on girl.

<table>
<tr><td>

Fondant

Blue

Brown

Red

Black

Green

</td><td>

Tools

Knife tool
Toothpick
2 x 6" skewer
White floral wire 6" long
¾" and 2¼" circle cutter
Cutting wheel
⅛" and ½" ball tool
½" square cutter
#2 round tip
Petal dust: peach, dark blue, brown
Food color: white

</td></tr>
</table>

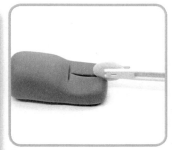

1 Take 2.75oz blue and roll to 3" sausage. Indent about half way down. Cut slit for pant legs and indent at top of slit to form top of legs front and back.

2 Use both index fingers to pinch along the top edge of pants to form a sharp edge.

3 Place skewer down center and indent a line down both sides of pant legs. Roll and cut ¼" x 2" strips for pant cuffs and glue on.

4 Roll .08oz brown into a 1" sausage. Indent twice with knife tool. Make two and glue to front of pant cuffs.

5 Roll .50oz into a red ball and flatten to fit top of overalls. Do not apply too much pressure on pants. Indent with your ½" square cutter for pocket placement.

6 Roll .50oz red into a 3" sausage and cut in half. Glue arms to sides with cut side down. Prop up one side with foam.

7 Roll 1.5oz brown into a circle, slightly flattened. Indent half way down with 2¼" circle cutter.

8 Use ⅛" ball tool to indent oval eyes, then ½" ball tool to indent oval nose, and a knife tool to indent muzzle. Use the circle to indent smile at base of muzzle line.

9 Roll some brown to ⅛" thick, cut (2) ¾" circles. Indent with ½" ball tool. Cut ¼ off each ear with circle cutter. Glue to head.

10 Repeat steps for feet to make hands, and make an indent on hand that is to hold fishing pole. Glue hands on and use 6" skewer for pole.

11 Cut a ¼" x 1" red strip for shirt detail and two small triangles for collar. Use #2 round tip for blue buttons. Roll black ⅛"oval eyes and ¼" oval nose. Add pocket detail.

12 Wrap white floral wire to top of fishing pole. Roll and cut a green teardrop and triangle shape. Glue together, add details, then glue fish to end of wire.

13 Use tiny ball tool to indent at corners of mouth for smile. Use white food color to paint a cross line pattern for shirt.

14 Add shading: brown — creases of feet, hands and all around muzzle; peach — cheeks, inner ears: blue - creases of pants and seams. Dot eyes with white.

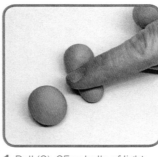

1 Roll (2) .25oz balls of light brown into 1" long sausages. Indent one half creating ball end. Make slight bend to create paw.

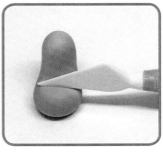

2 Stand upright on the ball end and create a crease with the back of your knife tool.

3 Insert a toothpick down the center, pushing into your foam support and indent twice on the front of the paw to form toes.

4 Repeat, but insert a 6" skewer through this leg and into the foam support. Roll a 1oz light brown ball into an egg shape and slide onto skewer.

5 Roll a ¼" brown ball of fondant into a teardrop and glue the larger end onto the back bottom side of your body for the tail.

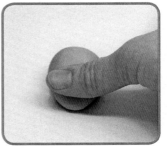

6 Roll a 1.25oz ball into an egg shape. Indent the smaller half slightly with thumb as this will create the muzzle of your puppy.

7 Mark a mouth line right in the center, then use your ½" ball tool to make an indent for nose and the ¼" ball tool for your eyes.

8 Glue puppy's head to top of body. Add small balls of black for the eyes and larger ball of black for the nose. The boy's nose can be a little larger than the girl's!

9 Roll a 1oz ball of pink into a teardrop shape and flatten slightly. Indent the larger end and form a heart shape. Glue to front of puppy.

10 Roll ½" ball of light brown fondant out to the thickness of ⅛". Cut (2) ½" ovals.

11 Glue the tip of your oval ear down just above eye area like shown. When secure you will then let the ear fold back down over itself.

12 Create the other ear and glue into place.

13 Roll (2) .10oz of light brown into tapered 1" long sausages. Indent and add details as with the feet. Glue to side of puppy, holding the heart.

14 Finish by adding details – white fondant on eyes, brown shading around paws and body, pink blush on cheeks. Paint on freckles, lashes and brows.

Fondant

Grey

Yellow

White

Peach

Black

Tools

5" skewer
⅛" ball tool
½" and 2" round cutters
#10 and #12 round tip

1 Body – roll 2oz of grey into egg shape and put skewer through middle.

2 Roll a .50oz grey sausage and cut in half. Flatten rounded end.

3 Glue flat side of each leg to the body.

4 Roll .40oz white to a sausage. Cut to 1". Cut end is bottom of bottle. From yellow, cut a ½"circle and roll a ¼" teardrop for nipple.

5 Roll 1.75oz in grey for the head, then start forming a teardrop.

6 Keep rolling, applying pressure towards the end to form a trunk about 1" long.

7 Lay head with trunk facing up and flatten top slightly and indent with both thumbs as shown. Also bend trunk up a bit.

8 Roll out .30oz grey for arms, cut in half, flatten rounded ends and attach to body.

9 Place bottle in center of arms and glue on. Glue head on. Indent with ball tool for eyes and roll and glue in black balls for eyes.

10 Roll a 1.5" ball of grey to 1/16" thick. Cut (2) 2" circles for ears. Using same cutter, cut a third away to form ear shape.

11 Glue ear to sides one at a time – hold in place for a few minutes to make sure it is adhered.

12 Roll a piece of white very thinly and use the #10 tip to cut 12 circles out. Trim each ¼" in from edge. Glue 3 toenails to each limb, cut side out and touching edge.

13 Cut ½"circle, then use #12 round tip to cut small circle. Roll a little sausage for handle and shape a small ball of peach into teardrop for nipple.

14 Add details with petal dust. Paint stripes on bottle, add white dots to eyes and paint on eyebrows.

Butterfly Buddies

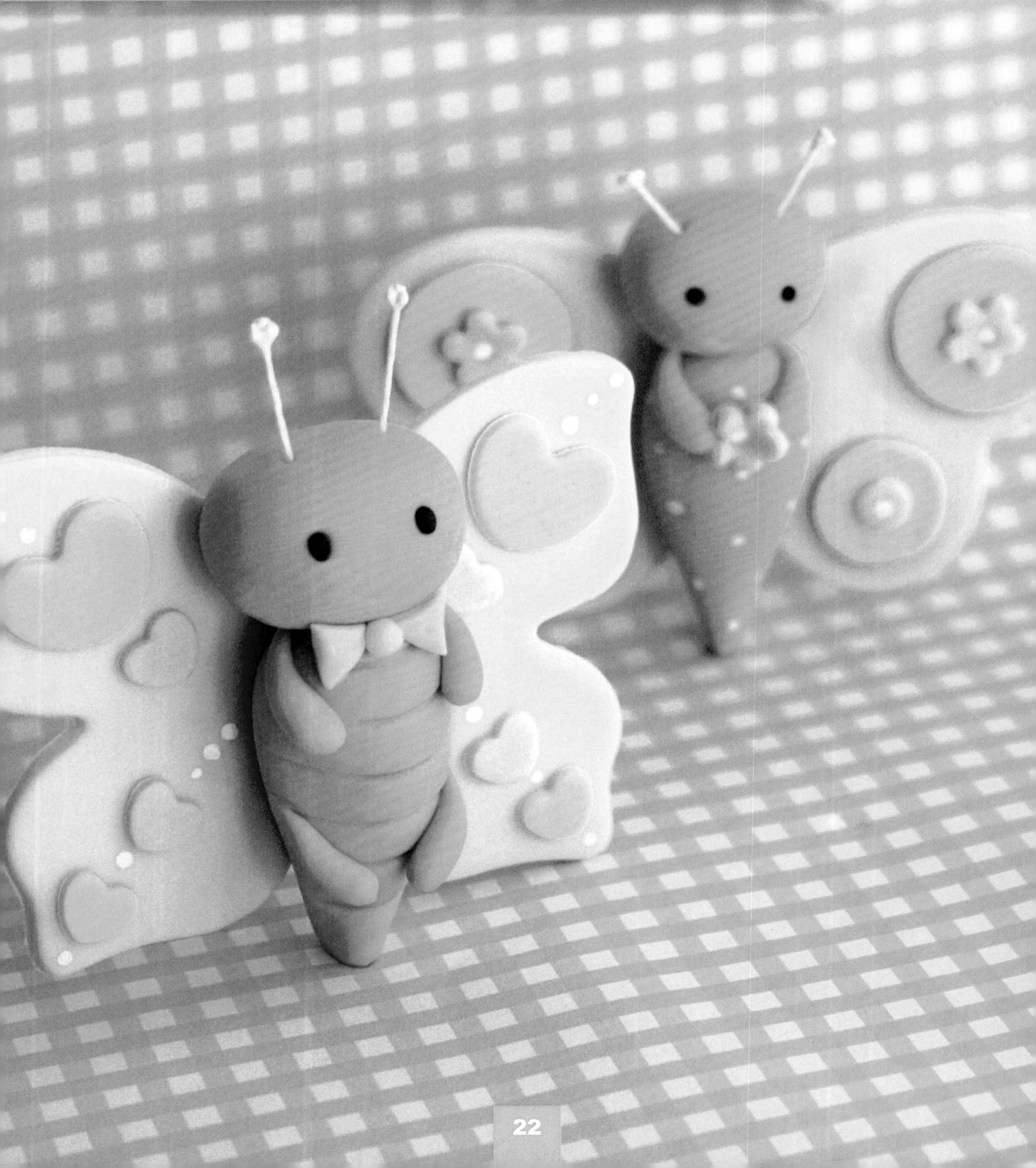

Fondant

Baby pink

Baby blue

Lavender

Green

Black

Tools

4" skewer

¼" triangle cutter

Heart cutter 3"

Butterfly cutter 3"

¼" and ½" heart cutters

Tiny ball tool

Small flower plunger cutter

White flower stamens

Petal dust: pink

Food color: white

1 Roll pink to ⅛" thickness. Use desired cutters to cut butterfly shape OR heart cutter to cut 2 wings.

2 Roll blue and lavender to ¹⁄₁₆" thick and cut two sizes of tiny hearts and glue to wings.

3 Roll blue and cut (2) ¾" & ½"circles. Glue to wings.

4 Roll .25oz of green into a 1.5" teardrop and insert 4" skewer.

5 Glue body to wings and use cutting wheel or blade tool to indent lines across body.

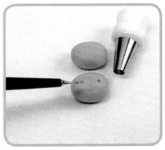

6 Roll .25oz green into a slight oval for head. Indent smile with #10 round tip and tiny ball tool for eyes.

7 Roll (4) ¼" balls into ½" long teardrops for arms and legs.

8 Glue arms and legs and head into place as shown.

9 For other butterfly, roll a smaller green body. No need to add indents on this body.

10 Repeat the same steps for head, slightly smaller. Glue onto body. Roll tiny black balls for eyes. Use a flower stamen for the antennae.

11 When using flower stamen, just cut in half and make sure you use a pin to indent a hole in the head where the stamen will be inserted.

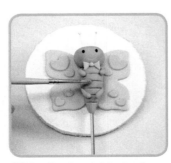

12 For the "male" butterfly, dust indents on body and cheeks with pink. See Bunny on page 9 for how to make a bow. Roll tiny black eyes.

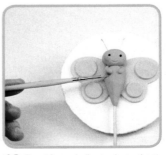

13 For "female" version, dust cheeks and vertically along body with pink. Add white dots to body along with tiny flower in center of hands.

14 Finishing touches. Add flowers to center of circles on female's wings. Add dots to the wings of male, as shown.

Fondant

Black

Yellow

Red

White

Tools

Toothpicks
2 x 6" skewers
½" oval cutter
Small square and rectangle cutters
#3 round tip
Veining tool
¼" ball tool
Petal dust: brown, grey
Floral wire: white
Food color: white

1 Roll out (2) .25oz balls of black to 1.5" long, and shape a bulbed end. Insert 6" skewer in one and toothpick in other.

2 Roll 1oz yellow into an egg shape, 1.5" tall, and glue to legs. Roll a ball of black to 4" long as thinly as possible. Cut (3) ¼" x 4" strips and glue to bee body.

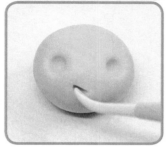

3 Roll a ball of white and cut 2 x medium oval shapes. Indent very slightly with cutter and fold back at indent. Set aside to dry.

4 Shape 1.5oz yellow into slightly oval head. Indent eyes with ¼" ball tool. Use large veining tool to indent mouth.

5 Roll (2) ¼" black balls for eyes and glue head to body.

6 Roll black to ¹⁄₁₆" thick and cut a 2.25" black circle. Glue and shape circle to top of head.

7 Cut (2) 1.5" white wire stems, and bend the ends. Roll ¼" black balls and glue to the bent ends.

8 Cut a small rectangle in white, ⅛" thick. Cut small black rectangle for screen. Use #3 tip for number keys and toothpick for holes for microphone.

9 Cut a long rectangle of red. Cut a thicker white rectangle and trim to book size. Wrap red around white to create book.

10 Glue book to side of bee. Glue side of cell phone to side of bee. Use foam to prop up until dry.

11 Roll .05oz black to 1.5" long, to make an arm. Shape a bulbed end. Make two.

12 Glue arms to sides of bee and onto book and cell phone. Leave the foam underneath until dry and sturdy.

13 Glue bent part of wings to the back sides of bee. Use brush to hold on for a minute until secure.

14 Dust pink on cheeks and in mouth. Dot eyes white. Insert antennae and paint words on book and dot numbers on cell. Dust cell number circles with grey.

Purrfectly Posh Kitty!

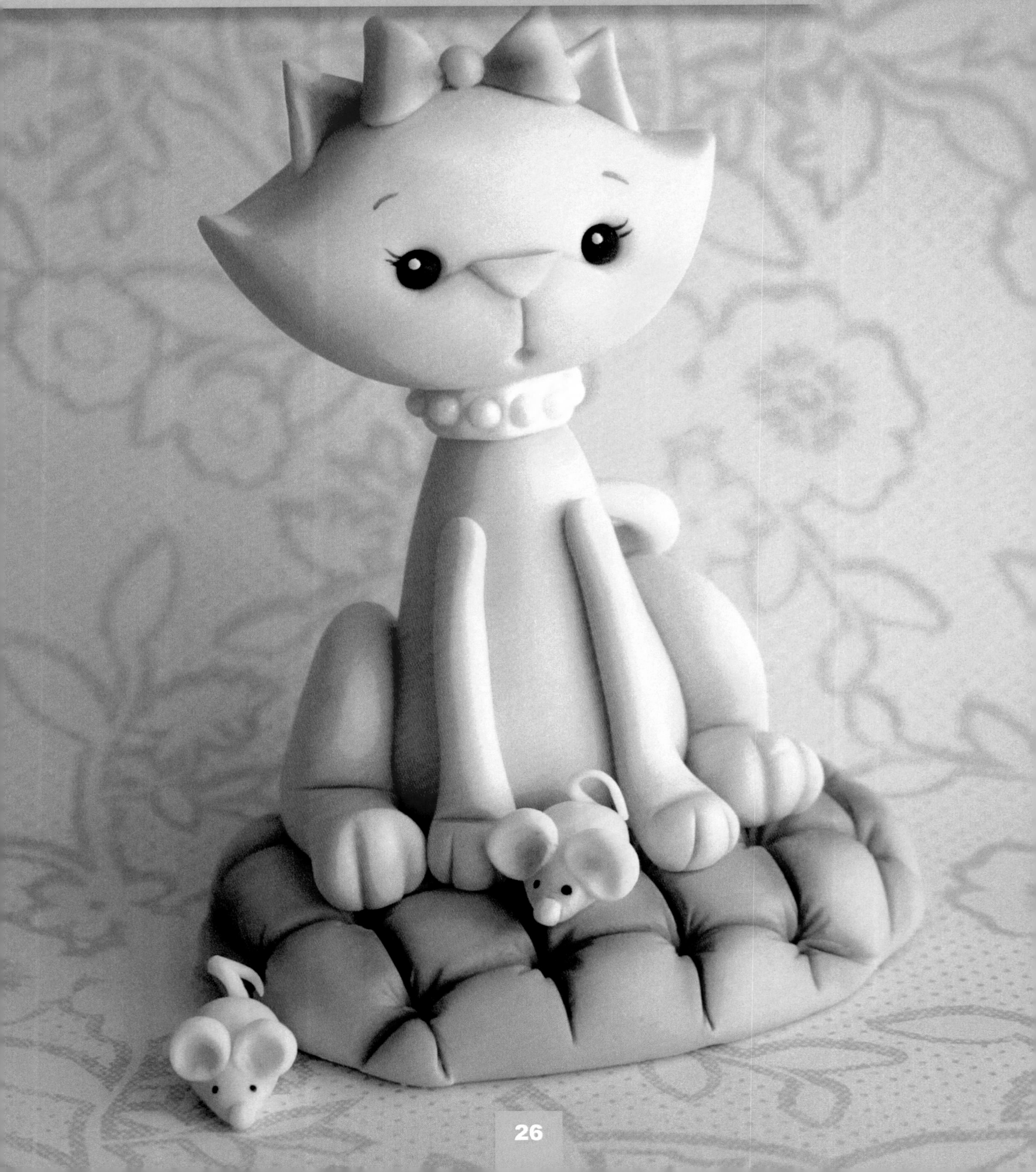

1 Roll 1.5oz of lavender into a flattened 3" circle. Indent with crossed lines, then use a star modeling tool to indent at intersections and form cushion.

2 Roll .25oz peach into a 1.5" drumstick shape. Flatten larger end. Turn upright and indent for toes and crease to form back legs. Make two.

3 Roll 1oz peach into a 2" tapered cone shape for body and insert 4.5" skewer. Glue to cushion. Glue both legs to sides.

4 Roll .05oz into a 2.25" long sausage. Glue onto back and bottom, forming a curve for tail.

5 Roll .05oz tapered into a 1.5" long sausage. Indent ends to form front paws and make crease for bend in paw. Glue to front of kitty and to cushion.

6 Roll a small white ball, flatten slightly and glue to top of body. Use 1/8" ball tool to indent all around, then glue sugar pearls all around collar.

7 For the head, roll 1oz peach to form a football shape. Softly pinch ends together and flatten slightly. Also flatten across main face area slightly.

8 Use a medium oval cutter to indent in center to form line for nose placement. Indent with 1/8" ball tool for eyes.

9 Indent line straight down from nose. Use tiny ball tool for mouth. Cut a pink triangle for nose. Roll small black balls for eyes.

10 Cut a peach 1/2" square. Cut square in half and bend together slightly to form ear.

11 Glue ears to head leaving 1/2" space in between. Make a lavender bow (see page 13) and glue in between ears. Glue head onto body.

12 For mice, shape a teardrop and indent tip with tiny ball tool. Add pink ball for nose. Roll tiny sausage for tail. Roll two balls for ears, indent with 1/8" ball tool.

13 Glue ears, tail and nose on mouse. Mouse can be any color you choose.

14 Add details with petal dust: peach – creases, base of ears; pink – ears, cheeks, nose, cushion and bow. Paint eyebrows and white dots on eyes. Dot black mice eyes.

1 Roll 2oz yellow into a 2.25" teardrop shape. Pinch tail upwards.

2 Roll a 1" ball of orange to 1/8" thick and cut (2) 7/8" circles. Use triangle to cut out 2 notches, forming feet.

3 Glue body to feet and insert toothpick in center of larger end of body.

4 Roll a 1.25oz yellow ball for head. Roll 1/4" and 1/3" balls to curved sausages for bill and glue on.

5 Cut 7/8" scallop in pink, then roll a .50oz pink ball and flatten. Indent with veining tool to make pleats. Glue with pleats at bottom to base.

6 Glue bonnet to head. Roll and glue small black balls for eyes. Glue head to body, centering on the toothpick.

7 Cut 2 yellow 2" leafs for wings. Use a 2" circle to round off large end of wing.

8 Glue wings onto both sides of body. Use veining tool to make wing detail. Indent 3 times.

9 Repeat steps to make smaller sized ducklings, using 1/2 to 1/3 the amount for mother duck. Glue heads with one looking up and one tilted.

10 Cover a cake base in green fondant and use the grass tip to stipple a "grass" look.

11 Roll a 1/2" ball of blue as thin as you can to any shape as this will be your pond. Glue to base.

12 Roll and cut a medium rectangle in green and use small triangle cutter to cut out various notches as shown.

13 Glue grass to edge of pond as shown.

14 Add details. Create bowtie and bow for ducklings (see page 13). Dust cheeks pink, wing edges and creases yellow. Dot white on bonnet and eyes.

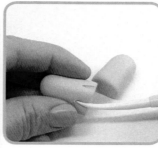

1 Roll .50oz lavender into 2" sausages, cut in half and indent twice with veining tool to create toes. Makes 2 legs.

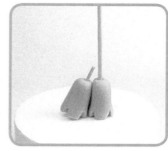

2 Insert a 5" skewer into one and a toothpick into other. Glue with legs touching and with one at an angle. Leave to dry.

3 Roll a 2oz lavender egg shape about 2" tall. Glue onto dried legs so they do not collapse.

4 Roll a 1.5" ball of blue to ¹⁄₁₆" and cut a 2" circle. Use #4 tip to cut out center.

5 Glue blue onto body and smooth it on. This is the shirt.

6 Roll .20oz blue into 1" football shape, cut in half. Indent cut end with ½"ball tool. Roll .15oz lavender into ball and cut in half. Indent to create fingers.

7 Glue arms to sides of hippo.

8 Roll 2.25oz egg shape 2" long for head. Indent smaller end by pressing about half way down. Press center of larger end with thumb to create mouth area.

9 Make an indent at top of mouth (under eye area). Use ⅛" ball tool to indent eyes. Use 1"circle to form mouth. Use ⅛" ball tool for nostrils and ends of smile.

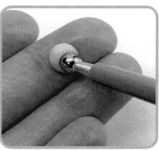

10 Roll ¼" lavender ball for ears. Indent with ¼" ball tool. Glue to top of head above eye areas.

11 Use veining tool to extend smile from indent to make "happy" expression. Use tiny ball tool to indent ends.

12 Roll ½"ball of green into a teardrop, indent end to form base of hat. Add small ball of pink for top of hat.

13 Cut a tiny circle for the cupcake base, then roll a long, thin sausage for the frosting. Twist the frosting and glue in place.

14 Add black balls for eyes and small white "teeth" on mouth. Add shading to features and paint on spots and stripes to shirt and hat. Add cupcake.

1 Roll .40oz grey into a 2" sausage, cut in half. Do this twice.

2 Insert a toothpick into each leg, cut side down. Place front and back two legs together with a ½" space between.

3 Roll 2.5oz of white into an oval and indent with small flower plunger OR large round tip for a 'fluffy' effect.

4 Center body over legs and glue on. Use the largest ball tool and indent a 1" circle at the front and top of body.

5 Roll a .75oz white ball and indent with thumb to make a groove on ⅔ of it.

6 Head will be slightly flattened, which is fine. Again, use flower plunger for detailing – around sides of face only.

7 Glue head onto the indented area.

8 Roll .25oz of grey into an oval and indent the top half slightly.

9 Use square cutter to indent nose in center of oval, knife tool down center to form mouth area, and indent eyes with ⅛" ball. Use tiny ball tool for mouth.

10 Glue face to head and add small black eyes.

11 Cut two white ½"circles. Fold one end together to form ear shape.

12 Glue ears to head with opening facing down. Roll a thin strip of pink and glue around neck. Add a small white teardrop for tail.

13 Create and glue a large pink bow (see page 13).

14 Dust black around bottom ⅛" of legs for hooves and grey around the center nose area. Dust pink on cheeks.

Fondant

- Light brown
- Dark brown
- Tan
- Black
- Green
- Yellow
- Light blue
- Dark blue
- Red

Tools

- Toothpicks
- 4" skewer
- 5" cake board
- ⅛" tiny ball tool
- 2" rectangle cutter
- ¾" round circle cutter
- Star plunger
- Bow mold
- 1.5" 5 petal flower cutter
- Small triangle cutter
- Grass tip
- Veining tool
- Food color: white, black
- Petal Dust: pink, brown, gold

1 Roll 4oz white to ⅛" thickness and larger than your 5" cake board. Trim around edge leaving about ½" extra around edge.

2 After gluing base to fondant, flip over and smooth all around cake base including sides.

3 Use grass tip to indent top and sides for a snow effect.

4 Roll dark brown fondant out to ½" x 2", add glue and wrap around a 4" skewer, leaving ½" at base. Make 2.

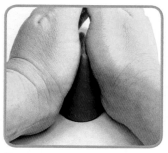

5 Roll 1oz green fondant to a 2" teardrop. Use palms and keep large end at base to roll against mat. This helps to create a flat bottom.

6 Make 2, slightly different heights, and add to your brown skewers.

7 Roll a 1.5" ball of light tan to ¹⁄₁₆" thick and cut out 2 flowers. Glue toothpick to the center as shown and glue both sides together for antlers.

8 Let antlers dry on a piece of foam.

9 Roll a 2oz piece of light brown into a thin 3" teardrop shape. Insert 4" skewer and glue to center of base.

10 Roll a 2" piece of dark brown to ½" thick. Cut out (4) ¾" circles.

11 Use knife tool to indent circle about ⅓ of the way in to create hooves.

12 Roll a 2" ball of light brown to a ½" thick sausage roll. Cut out (4) 2" sausages.

13 Leaving a ½" in the center, roll slightly on either side until sausage is 2.5" long for leg.

14 Pinch one end of leg, this will be the end glued to body. Do this to all 4 pieces.

 **15** First glue legs to both sides of body as shown THEN glue to base.

 **16** Glue hooves onto legs with indent slightly facing outwards.

 **17** Glue two other hooves in front of body and not going past the back legs.

 **18** Glue front leg to body first and then bend slightly and glue bottom of leg to hoof.

 **19** Repeat for other side.

 **20** Roll 1oz ball of light blue to 2" sausage and roll to ⅛" thickness. Set aside, covered.

 **21** Roll a .25oz ball of red to a 3" sausage as thinly as possible.

 **22** Use ruler to cut two strips of ¼" x length of red.

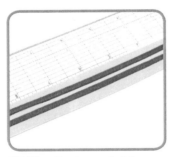 **23** Glue the two red strips evenly onto blue.

 **24** Roll again to make a ¹⁄₁₆" or less thickness. Trim scarf to 1" x 8" total length after rolling.

 **25** Use your knife to cut ¾" strips into both ends of scarf.

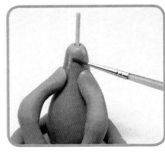 **26** Glue around top of neck only.

 **27** Wrap scarf around neck and slightly onto legs.

 **28** You may use a piece of foam to prop up some curves until dry enough to hold its shape.

 **29** Roll 2oz light brown to a 2" peanut shape. Indent smaller top end slightly.

 **30** When looking at piece straight on, the indented part will be the eye area.

31 Use ⅛" ball tool to indent eyes close together, about ¾" down from top of head. Indent two ovals for nostrils.

32 Glue head on with the mouth area hanging over the front of the body.

33 Now indent mouth area with the same ⅛" ball tool.

34 Roll a ½"ball of light brown to ¹⁄₁₆" thick and cut (2) ¾" circles. Glue together close to bottom to form ear.

35 Flatten glued end with ear opening facing down.

36 Glue ears onto head at just about eye level.

37 Use toothpick to indent right above ears on either slide to make antlers easy to insert.

38 Insert dried antlers at just a slight angle upwards on both sides. Roll small black balls for eyes or use 4mm black sugar pearls.

39 Roll a ball of red and light blue to ½" to ¾" thickness and use the rectangle cutter to create several sizes of presents.

40 Roll a ½"ball of yellow to ⅛" thick and use large star plunger to cut 2 stars for tops of trees.

41 Roll ¼" blue to teardrop shape and turn up small end to form bird shape. Use #10 cutter to indent wings.

42 Roll a tiny pinch of yellow to a teardrop for bird's beak.

43 Roll several tiny red balls and glue all around the trees.

44 Paint presents with white and gold lines and dots.

45 Insert trees behind moose and add presents next to him. Glue one bird carefully to an antler and another to one hoof.

46 Roll ⅛" balls of brown to teardrops for eyebrows. Dust details. Dot bird eyes black. Add bows on various presents.

1 Roll 3oz of brown to ⅛" thick to a size a little larger than 5" cake board. Use a woodgrain texture mat across piece and match up seams.

2 Brush edible glue or water across surface of cake board.

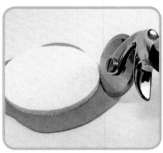

3 Gently face woodgrain side down. Apply wet side of cake board down, press gently. Use pizza cutter or sharp knife and cut along edge.

4 Flip board over and your cake board is complete.

5 Take .25oz of brown and begin rolling a sausage with a ball end totaling 2.5" long. Make 2 of these.

6 Pinch ball end to flatten slightly.

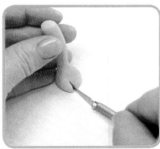

7 Stand up on flat foot and cut ¼" from end to form thumb/toe. Cut opposite side for other foot.

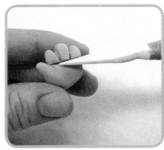

8 Use knife tool to indent 2 more toes and then again at base of foot underneath toes.

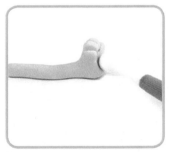

9 Use ½" ball tool to indent base of foot.

10 Glue onto board, starting about 2" from the back and leaving a 1" space between legs at the back.

11 Roll 1.5oz brown into a pear shape, slightly tilted forward. Insert skewer and glue to base in between the legs.

12 Roll 2oz black to ⅟₁₆" thick. Cut a 3¼" x 1½" rectangle. Use medium diamond and small square to trim corners as shown.

13 Glue jacket onto body with larger cut end at top and wrap around.

14 Roll and cut a medium white triangle. Cut triangle in half.

 **15** Glue white shirt piece into place in center opening as shown.

 **16** For each hand, roll a tapered egg shape in brown. Indent larger end with thumb. Use knife to cut 3 times for fingers.

 **17** Gently roll each end to form fingers.

 **18** Indent little wrinkles across fingers with knife tool and use 1/8" ball to indent for fingernails.

 **19** Roll .30oz black into 4" sausage and cut in half for arms. Indent cut end with ball tool.

 **20** Glue right hand to board in front of body in between legs. (closer to right leg) Glue arm to hand and side of body.

 **21** Glue left arm to body and rest on sponge. Glue hand to arm and use toothpick to wrap fingers around, for placement only. (do not glue toothpick).

 **22** Roll 1.75oz brown into a 2" wide oval for head.

 **23** Roll a 1" ball of tan to 1/16" thick. Cut a 1¾" circle and use 2" heart cutter to trim the indent for face.

 **24** Smooth around edges of cut face and glue to top of oval. Use thumb to slightly indent top half of face.

 **25** Roll 1/8" oval and glue to center of face. Indent two nostrils with tiny ball tool.

 **26** Use tiny ball tool to indent mouth opening and oval eyes.

 **27** Using same small ball tool, gently indent underneath mouth to form chin and expression.

 **28** Cut (2) 1¼" ovals. Using same cutter trim off 1/3" from each oval to form both lapels for jacket.

 **29** Glue lapels onto either side of jacket with curve facing center as shown.

 **30** Cut two medium red diamonds and fold in half to form bow. Roll a small oval for center of bow.

31 Glue bow parts in place. Glue head on. Roll 2 small black ovals for eyes.

32 Roll a 1" ball of brown to ⅛" thick. Cut (2) ¾"circles. Roll 1" ball of tan very thinly and cut (2) ¾" circles and glue on top. Trim as shown.

33 Use ½" ball tool to indent centers of both ears.

34 Glue ears to sides of head, half way up.

35 Roll .50oz black into 1" oval. Use both palms of hand and roll oval gently, pressing on surface as you roll.

36 Flip oval over and you will have the "top" part of your top-hat.

37 Cut a 1½" circle, ⅛"thick. Glue top of hat to circle base and use a piece of paper towel under each side to prop up while drying.

38 Roll a 1" ball of white as thinly as possible and cut a 2.5" x ¼" strip. Glue onto hat base and use a soft brush to form and smooth.

39 Use toothpick and poke hole in top of head. Insert toothpick into bottom of hat and glue on head titled to one side.

40 Cut 4 small buttons in grey using a #3 or #4 round tip. Glue to jacket front and to cuffs of sleeves.

41 Roll a ½" brown ball to 3" long tail and shape as desired. Glue to back end and base.

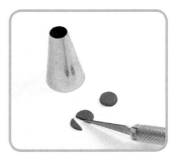

42 Use a #12 round tip to cut 2 dark brown circles. Trim off edge. Glue to base of foot, trimmed edge up.

43 Roll 2 tiny dark brown sausages for eyebrows. Glue above eyes creating arch.

44 Use a medium rectangle to cut 4 white playing cards. Paint card details with red food color.

45 Make 3 red balls. Glue cards in place. Use black edible marker to paint toothpick. Use silver sheen to paint ends of magic wand and buttons.

46 Do all shading. Paint inside of mouth black. Use a #10 round tip to make some coins and paint gold.

1 Roll 1.5oz tan and 1oz white and flatten slightly on one end.

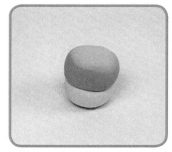

2 Glue both flattened ends together.

3 Roll together and then form a cone shape with base of hand.

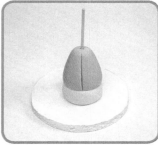

4 Inset 4" skewer in center and use knife tool to indent down front of tan part.

5 Roll a .25oz black 1" oval and a .05oz black ½" sausage. Indent sausage twice, forming paw, and glue. Make 2.

6 Glue both leg/paw combination to sides of white body.

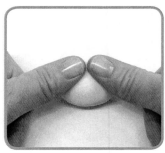

7 Roll a 1.5oz white circle for head and use thumbs at an angle to slightly indent for face.

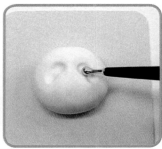

8 At indented area, use ¼" ball tool to create a kidney shape for eyes totaling ½" long.

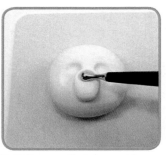

9 Roll a small white oval for muzzle. Indent an oval area for nose with ¼" ball tool.

10 Use knife tool and indent straight down from nose area. Roll black slight teardrop shapes for eyes and an oval for nose. Glue in place.

11 Once all black is glued into place use an ⅛" ball tool and indent eye area and mouth area.

12 Roll a piece of white to 1/16" thick. Use 1" diamond cutter, then trim away both sides of diamond forming tie shape.

13 Glue tie to front of tan body and make a ⅛" ball into triangle shape to finish off tie.

14 Make (2) black 1.5" long bulbed sausage shapes in black. Indent twice at end and once across top to form paw.

15 Glue arms to side with indents facing out. Glue head onto body. Make small black ball eyes OR use 4mm black sugar pearls.

16 Roll two black balls for ears. Indent with ½" ball tool.

17 Trim off edge of ears.

18 Glue ears to head.

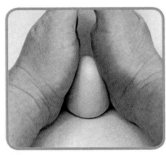

19 Now for the Bride! Roll a 2oz white ball into a cone shape.

20 Flatten top of cone until skirt is 1½" tall. Use veining tool to make creases around skirt.

21 Insert a 4" skewer to center of skirt.

22 Roll two black ½" sausages. Indent twice to form paw. Glue paws to front bottom of skirt.

23 Roll a .50oz white flattened circle for bodice.

24 Glue bodice to skirt.

25 Roll a 1" piece of tan to ⅛" thick and cut a ¼"x 3" piece and glue around waist.

26 Roll two black arms, each a 1.5" long bulbed sausage. Indent twice at large end to form paw and once across top.

27 Glue arms to body making sure to leave at least ¼" in center.

28 Roll 4oz of white to an ⅛" thickness and use any impression mat of choice.

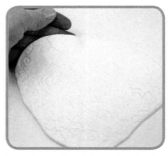

29 Carefully pick up fondant and flip over impression side down.

30 Cover your cake board with glue.

 **31** You now have a lovely covered cake board with an impression.

 **32** Gently press glue side down onto fondant and use pizza cutter or knife to trim off around edge.

 **33** Glue both pandas to cake board side by side. If needed, trim off excess skewer so it doesn't go through top of head when placed on body.

 **34** Roll a .05oz green 1" sausage. Use cutting tool or knife to make several lines to represent stems.

 **35** Glue stems to center of body between paws.

 **36** Make a .05oz white ball and glue to top of stems. This will be the base of the flowers.

 **37** Use your small flower plunger with white 1/16" thick fondant and fill the ball with flowers.

 **38** Roll a 1/16" size green teardrop and flatten for boutenierre leaf.

 **39** Add flower to boutenierre.

 **40** Repeat steps for making head for boy panda EXCEPT use a 1" circle cutter to indent a smile for your girl panda.

 **41** Glue girl head on. They should be equally tall.

 **42** Add a 1/4" oval black ball to back of boy for tail.

 **43** Roll some white to 1/8" thick. Use largest flower plunger and trim off 2 leaves to form a tiara. Use toothpick to indent tiny dots.

 **44** Make 1/16" size white teardrops to add as accents for tiara. Glue to top of head.

 **45** Roll lots of tiny specks of yellow and fill in all centers of flowers.

 **46** Finish by dusting pink cheeks and inside of boys mouth. Use #3 round tip and create buttons for his vest.

1 Use brown fondant and a small hole adapter in extruder gun. Extrude enough to cover edge of a 2" circle twice.

2 Cut a ⅛" thick 2" brown circle and glue two layers of extruded strings along edge.

3 Roll 2.35oz tan into a 2½" egg shape. Indent center of top of egg and pinch fingers together at edges, forming ears.

4 Lay on back and flatten face area slightly with thumb. For mama owl repeat steps using 2.25oz light tan.

5 Use .25oz tan and light tan for each baby owl. Hold between fingers as shown and indent with other finger to form ears.

6 Roll matching color for wings. Use any impression mat and then use a 1" and ½" leaf cutter for wings.

7 Glue various embossed wings onto bodies.

8 Roll white fondant to ⅛" thick and cut ¾" circles & #12 tip circles for eyes of adults and babies. Indent slightly with large ball tool.

9 Roll muted yellow to ⅛" thick and cut out small triangle. Trim ¼" edge off to form beak.

10 Glue eyes onto head and beak onto eyes with beak matching up with base of eyes. Indent ⅛" balls for eyes. Roll small black balls for eyes.

11 Roll out pink and cut medium and small triangle. Cut off both sides as shown to form ties. Roll small balls to top off ties for both sized owls.

12 Roll two green stems and glue to body. Roll 2 small teardrops and indent center with veining tool for leaf.

13 Glue ties onto body as shown. Use small flower plunger and glue flowers onto top of stems and a few on top of head.

14 Glue babies to nest. You can roll a small ball to place under one to make a little higher. Dust cheeks and tips of wings and ears with pink.

Made in the USA
San Bernardino, CA
17 March 2015